W9-BWU-531

Sacco and Vanzetti

CORNERSTONES OF FREEDOM

SECOND SERIES

Elaine Landau

Children's Press®
A Division of Scholastic Inc.
New York • Toronto • London • Auckland • Sydney
Mexico City • New Delhi • Hong Kong
Danbury, Connecticut

Photographs © 2004: Courtesy of the Trustees of the Boston Public Library: 5, 23, 25 bottom, 26, 29; Brown Brothers: 6 bottom, 33, 36 left, 44 bottom right, 44 bottom left, 45 top; Corbis Images: cover bottom, 20, 21, 25 top, 27, 28, 31, 32, 40, 41, 45 bottom (Bettmann), 11, 12 (Underwood & Underwood); Culver Pictures: 10; Franklin Watts Photo Archive: 8; Harvard Law Library, courtesy of Art and Visual Materials, Special Collections Department: 17 top, 17 bottom, 22, 34, 35, 44 top left, 44 top right; Hulton|Archive/Getty Images: 13 bottom, 13 top; Courtesy of Massachusetts State Archives, Boston: 3, 4, 6 top, 7, 30 (Judicial Archives, Exhibit, Comm. V Sacco and Vanzetti), 24, 38, 39 (PR27-PO28X), 36 right, 37 (PS11-2084X); Merlin-Net, Inc.: 18 (The Boston Globe via www.Merlin-Net.com); Old Bridgewater Historical Society, MA: 16; The Image Works/Topham: cover top, 15.

Library of Congress Cataloging-in-Publication Data

Landau, Elaine.

  Sacco and Vanzetti / Elaine Landau.

    p. cm. — (Cornerstones of freedom. Second series)

  Summary: Tells the story of Italian immigrants Nicola Sacco and Bartolomeo Vanzetti, who were tried for murder in a political climate that greatly affected their right to a fair trial.

  Includes bibliographical references and index.

    ISBN 0-516-24237-7

    1. Sacco, Nicola, 1891–1927—Trials, litigation, etc.—Juvenile literature. 2. Vanzetti, Bartolomeo, 1888–1927—Trials, litigation, etc.—Juvenile literature. 3. Trials (Murder)—Massachusetts—Juvenile literature. [1. Sacco, Nicola, 1891–1927—Trials, litigation, etc. 2. Vanzetti, Bartolomeo, 1888–1927—Trials, litigation, etc. 3. Trials (Murder)] I. Title. II. Series.

KF224.S2L36 2004

345.73'02523—dc22

                                                    2003016940

I T WAS LATE AFTERNOON ON April 15, 1920, in South Braintree, Massachusetts, a small industrial town south of Boston. The staff at Slater and Morrill Shoe Factories had just finished preparing the last employee pay envelopes. The only thing left to do was for **paymaster** Frederick A. Parmenter to bring the money to the company's other building to make sure the workers got their pay. The other building was only about 200 yards (182 meters) away, and he could have easily walked there on his own. However, because he would be carrying about $16,000, the company guard, Alessandro Berardelli, went with him.

* * * *

Walking down Pearl Street toward their destination, Parmenter and Berardelli passed a group of Italian workers. The workers were busy laying the foundation for a new restaurant. No one paid any attention to two men, standing nearby, dressed in black, who were not part of the crew, until one of them suddenly reached out and grabbed Berardelli.

After that, things seemed to happen at the speed of a runaway train. The second man pulled out a gun and shot Berardelli three times. Then he turned and shot Parmenter. Parmenter, who was still able to walk, staggered toward the workers. The gunman shot him again, and Parmenter fell.

On the afternoon of April 15, 1920, Parmenter and Berardelli left the Slater and Morrill office, shown here, for the last time.

This photograph shows the scene of the shooting on Pearl Street.

Berardelli, who had fallen in the street, tried climbing to his knees but was unable to stand. The gunman shot him two more times.

At that point, two men in a Buick pulled up to the crime scene. It was the getaway car. Seeing it, the two criminals snatched up the tin payroll boxes and jumped into the car. A third man—part of the criminals' backup team—quickly joined them. The Buick pulled away and was out of sight

In a daring escape, the getaway car managed to throw off police after crossing these railroad tracks.

Police officers tried to solve the case by recreating the scene of the attack.

within seconds. Yet their getaway was not as smooth as they had hoped. The police had been alerted and were now after them. It looked as if the authorities were closing in when the Buick reached the railroad tracks.

The railroad guardrail had just gone down, meaning that a train was coming. But the robbers were willing to take their chances. Pulling out his gun, one of them yelled to the gatekeeper to raise the guardrail. The frightened gatekeeper did as he was told, and the Buick's driver stepped on the gas.

The car made it safely across, but the robbers weren't leaving anything to chance. Earlier, they had prepared long strips of rubber with nails sticking through them. Now they threw these out behind their car. The idea was to deflate the tires of the police cars following them. As it turned out, that wasn't necessary. The men managed to avoid the police, and the authorities were left with the task of solving the crime.

THE INVESTIGATION

Although there were **witnesses** to the South Braintree robbery and murders, the police didn't have much to go on. They learned that the Buick used as the getaway car had been stolen in November of the previous year. The authorities suspected that the stolen vehicle had been used in another crime as well. The car's description fit that of one used in a botched robbery attempt on Christmas Eve in nearby Bridgewater, Massachusetts. That morning, two armed men attacked the White Shoe Company's payroll truck. The truck, which held nearly $30,000 in cash, was also carrying a driver, the paymaster, and an armed guard. When the robbers shot at the truck, the payroll guard fired back. Then bullets seemed to fly in all directions. Realizing that they were not going to succeed, the robbers fled the scene in the stolen Buick.

It was widely believed that this stolen Buick was used in both the South Braintree and Bridgewater crimes.

This is a map of the area around the crime scene in South Braintree. The site of the shooting on Pearl Street is marked with an "X."

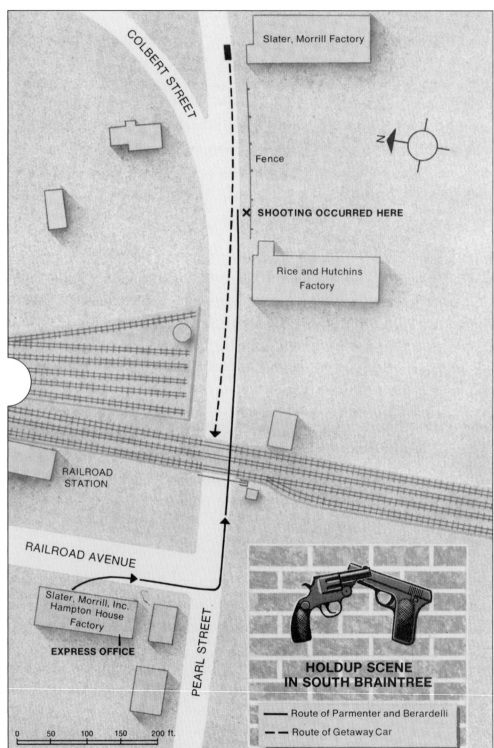

COLBERT STREET

Slater, Morrill Factory

N

Fence

X SHOOTING OCCURRED HERE

Rice and Hutchins Factory

RAILROAD STATION

RAILROAD AVENUE

Slater, Morrill, Inc.
Hampton House
Factory

EXPRESS OFFICE

PEARL STREET

**HOLDUP SCENE
IN SOUTH BRAINTREE**

——— Route of Parmenter and Berardelli

- - - Route of Getaway Car

0   50   100   150   200 ft.

It had been a close call for the men in the White Shoe Company truck. When the robbers first began firing at them, the driver momentarily lost control of the truck and hit a telegraph pole. However, the robbers' bullets missed them and they managed to save the payroll.

The police suspected that the stolen Buick probably used in both holdups was an important clue. Unfortunately, the police didn't get much of a description of the criminals in either case. At first, most of the witnesses only said the robbers looked "dark and foreign." Nevertheless, from that small bit of information, the police made some important conclusions that greatly affected the case.

Michael Stewart, the Bridgewater police chief, soon settled on a profile, or a list of characteristics that he felt fit the culprits. From the descriptions he heard, Stewart believed that they were probably Italian **immigrants** who were political radicals—people willing to use extreme measures to bring about change in society. That might seem like quite a stretch. However, many people believe that the police chief, along with other people connected to the case, were greatly influenced by the political climate of the times.

During that period, there had been a flood of Italian immigrants into the United States. Other immigrant groups, which had been in the United States longer and thought of themselves as "real" Americans, were suspicious of these newcomers, who spoke a different language and had seemingly strange customs and views. Often,

A group of Italian immigrants await entry to the United States at Ellis Island. Like other immigrants, the Italians faced many hardships and prejudice upon their arrival in this country.

ITALIAN IMMIGRATION

Between 1880 and 1920, nearly four million Italians came to the United States to live. Most arrived hoping to build a better life for themselves and for their families. Often, they would settle along the East Coast, in cities such as New York and Boston, where they created neighborhoods bursting with Italian restaurants, cafes, and shops. These areas became known as "Little Italy."

Italian American immigrants were unfairly blamed for everything from the lack of jobs available to various criminal activities.

At times, this **prejudice** threatened the fairness of the U.S. legal system. In the United States, everyone, no matter where he or she comes from, is considered innocent until proven guilty. When a police chief or others in the legal system decide that someone is guilty of a crime simply because of that person's **ethnicity** or political views, it becomes more difficult for that person to get a fair trial. It has already been decided that he or she is guilty.

✳ ✳ ✳ ✳

THE RED SCARE, 1919–1920

Prejudice against Italian Americans peaked from 1919 to 1920. This was an unsettling period in U.S. history known as the "Red Scare." In 1920, Americans had just finished fighting in World War I. They had seen what was happening in other parts of the world and didn't like much of it. Americans had heard about the 1917 Russian Revolution, in which discontented workers overthrew the government and established a **communist** (Red) society. In a communist society, private ownership of stores, hotels, manufacturing plants, and other businesses does not exist. Instead, all of

Soldiers in the Russian Revolution celebrated their victory in 1917, which led to a communist society in Russia.

these are held in "common," which means they are equally held among the people as a whole.

People in the United States were highly suspicious of communists. In the United States, most businesses are privately owned. People are expected to get ahead through their own ability and effort, not because the government distributed the nation's wealth equally. Most Americans did not want communists in the United States to stir up workers and encourage them to revolt. Many Americans were also wary of **anarchists**, people who are against any form of government or business ownership by large corporations. Such political beliefs were considered "un-American" by many. In 1919–1920, patriotism was the order of the day in the United States.

A group of Russian farm workers posed for this picture in the 1920s. Large farms such as this one were run by state officials.

Due to a fear of communism spreading in the United States, raids were carried out against anyone or anything seen as a threat to our government. At left, Boston police haul away suspicious books. Below, local police destroyed a Union of Russians office in the United States.

At times, these patriotic feelings were carried to an extreme. Labor unions that held strikes to try and improve working conditions were seen as serious threats to the country. Some people thought giving workers too much power could hurt U.S. businesses or even lead to a communist takeover. In some cases, labor leaders, anarchists, and others were accused of being **traitors**. Some people were even arrested for speaking out against the government or U.S. business principles.

THE ARREST

These kinds of fears set the tone for the police investigation. At first, authorities weren't sure whether the getaway car had been a Buick or a similar-looking vehicle called a Hudson Overland. However, Police Chief Stewart knew an Italian named Mike Boda (also known as Mario Buda) who owned an Overland. Boda shared a house with another Italian named Ferruccio Coacci.

Coacci, who had been served **deportation** papers (he was asked to leave the country), had failed to show up for his deportation hearing. The fact that Coacci had been asked to leave the United States, along with Boda's ownership of a car that looked like the getaway vehicle, made them both **suspects** in the eyes of the police. Although the two men could show that they were somewhere else at the times of the crimes, Chief Stewart was still suspicious.

On April 17, just two days after the South Braintree crime, Mike Boda brought his Overland to the Elm Square Garage for repairs.

In part because they were Italian immigrants, local police were prejudiced against Sacco (right) and Vanzetti (left) from the start.

★ ★ ★ ★

S., FRIDAY, MAY 14, 1920

Believe They Have White Bandits

With the arrest at Brockton the latter part of last week of three men upon whom it is hoped to fix the responsibility for the robbery of the Slater & Morrill pay roll of $20,000 and the killing of the paymaster and his guard at South Braintree April 15, the local police believe they have secured at last one of the men who attempted to hold up the L. Q. White factory pay roll on Broad street in this town last December. Officer Benjamin Bowles, who guarding Paymaster Cox at the t and several persons who were on t street in the vicinity, are sure that Bartholomew Vanzetti of Plymouth, one of the men under arrest, was the man who knelt on the ground and discharged a shot gun several times at the men on the truck which was conveying the money from the bank of the Bridgewater Trust Company to the factory. Chief of Police Stewart has been very active and has rendered valuable aid to the State and Brockton officers before and since these men were taken into custody. He hopes also to connect Nichol Sacco of Stoughton, another of the prisoners, with the White affair.

A newspaper headline announces the arrest of Sacco and Vanzetti.

HOW DID THEY WIND UP HERE?

At the time of their arrest, Nicola Sacco and Bartolomeo Vanzetti had only been in the United States for twelve years. After arriving separately from Italy, both settled in Massachusetts. Sacco found work in a shoe factory and later married. The couple had one child. Vanzetti first worked as a cook and then as a factory worker. He later found steady work selling fish in a Plymouth, Massachusetts fish market.

Stewart heard about this and told the garage owner, Simon Johnson, to call the police when Boda came to pick up his car. Chief Stewart thought Boda might be part of the gang that committed the Bridgewater and South Braintree crimes. He was anxious to see who came with him to pick up the car.

The chief's trap worked. Mike Boda did not come for his car alone. On the evening of May 5, 1920, three of Boda's friends met him at the garage. The garage was closed, so they went to Simon Johnson's house. Two of the men who had arrived there by streetcar were twenty-nine-year-old Nicola Sacco and thirty-two-year-old Bartolomeo Vanzetti. Both were Italian immigrants who had attended anarchist meetings and sometimes passed out anarchist flyers. That alone would have made them suspect during the Red Scare, but knowing Boda made things even worse for them.

Though Boda and his friends expected to leave in the Overland, the garage owner told the men that he could not return the car because it did not have current license plates. Meanwhile, his wife quietly phoned the police. The four Italians left, unaware that the police had been alerted. Sacco and Vanzetti got back on the streetcar and, after they had stopped at a few stations, two police officers got on board. Looking for a pair of fellows they later described as "the Italians," they arrested Sacco and Vanzetti.

16

AT THE POLICE STATION

At the police station, both men were questioned without an attorney (lawyer) present. At first, the men didn't know what the police wanted with them. Neither had been anywhere near South Braintree or Bridgewater at the time the crimes were committed. Instead, they suspected that their political views might have landed them in trouble.

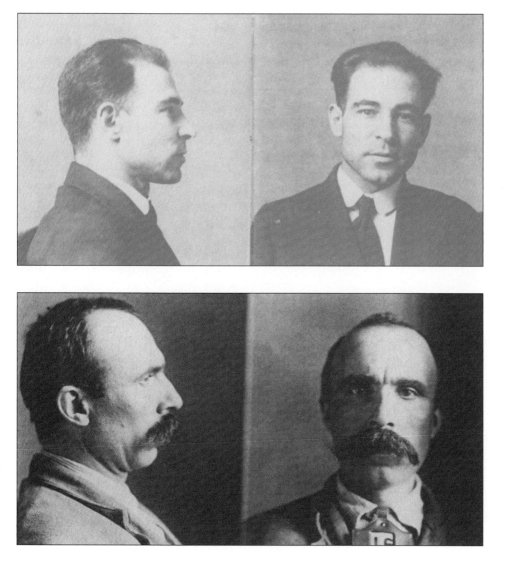

These mug shots of Sacco (top) and Vanzetti (bottom) were taken upon their arrest.

17

Frightened, the pair tried to cover up their political activities. When arrested, both men were carrying fully loaded guns. They needed these weapons for their own protection. It was common for anarchists to be attacked by angry mobs claiming to be patriots. In some cases, anarchists had even been unlawfully attacked by the police.

At times, Sacco and Vanzetti also needed to be armed for work-related reasons. Sacco sometimes worked as the night watchman at the shoe factory where he was employed. He needed a gun to guard the area. Vanzetti also needed a weapon on days when he took in a lot of

Sacco and Vanzetti are shown here in the prisoner's cage. They both lied to the police when questioned, even though they did not know why they had been arrested.

cash selling fish. Being armed kept the robbers away. Now the men felt sure the police would think their guns were being used for criminal purposes. Therefore, they lied about where they had gotten their weapons.

The men also lied about who their friends were and whether they belonged to any anarchist groups. They claimed they did not know Mike Boda or his roommate Coacci, even though they were arrested after meeting Boda that night. The men were afraid and did not want to look guilty, but their lies did not prove helpful.

Sacco and Vanzetti faced another round of questioning the next day. By then, the case seemed to center around Mike Boda's friends and acquaintances. Because his car was thought to be used in the crimes, anyone he knew was seen as a possible gang member. Even after the actual stolen Buick used in the crime was found in the woods, the police still believed that Boda and his friends were connected to the crimes. The wooded area in which the car had been found was only a few miles from Boda's home.

THE HIGH PRICE OF PREJUDICE

Unfortunately, prejudice on the part of the police, the court system, and the public would work against Sacco and Vanzetti. As historian and Harvard University professor Arthur Schlesinger wrote, "It must be remembered that Sacco and Vanzetti were immigrants, they were poor, they were atheists [did not believe in God], they were draft dodgers, they were anarchists. They were exactly the kind of person who 100% Americans [people who saw themselves as every inch American] felt might be guilty of anything."

The police also focused on Boda's roommate, Ferruccio Coacci. Coacci said that he'd missed his deportation hearing because his wife had been ill. After investigating, the police found that Coacci's wife was in perfect health. On April 16, 1920, the authorities arrived at Coacci's

Many anarchists, or "Reds," like Coacci were deported, or forced to leave the United States. Here, a group of Reds await deportation at Ellis Island in 1920.

home to bring him to the immigration center. After two days, he was put on a boat to Italy. The police were glad to see him go.

With Coacci gone, the police turned their attention to Mike Boda. To escape certain arrest and prosecution, Boda went into hiding. Some claim he went back to Italy and never returned. Others believe he remained in hiding in the United States.

Either way, that left Sacco and Vanzetti as the best suspects. Sacco was able to prove that he worked at the 3-K Shoe Factory all day on December 24, so he could not be connected to the Bridgewater incident. Yet he had taken the day off on April 15. That opened the door for him to be charged with the South Braintree robbery and murders.

✳ ✳ ✳ ✳

Sacco had a good reason for not being at work that day. He had been planning a trip back to Italy to see his family. The trip was important to him because his mother had recently died, and he wanted to be with the rest of his family. Sacco also wanted them to meet Rosina, an Italian girl he'd married in the United States. He hoped to bring their young son Dante along as well.

This Sacco family portrait, taken in 1920, shows Nicola Sacco with his wife, Rosina, and his son, Dante.

Sacco's passport, shown here, was used during the trial as proof that Sacco had gone to Boston on the day of the robbery.

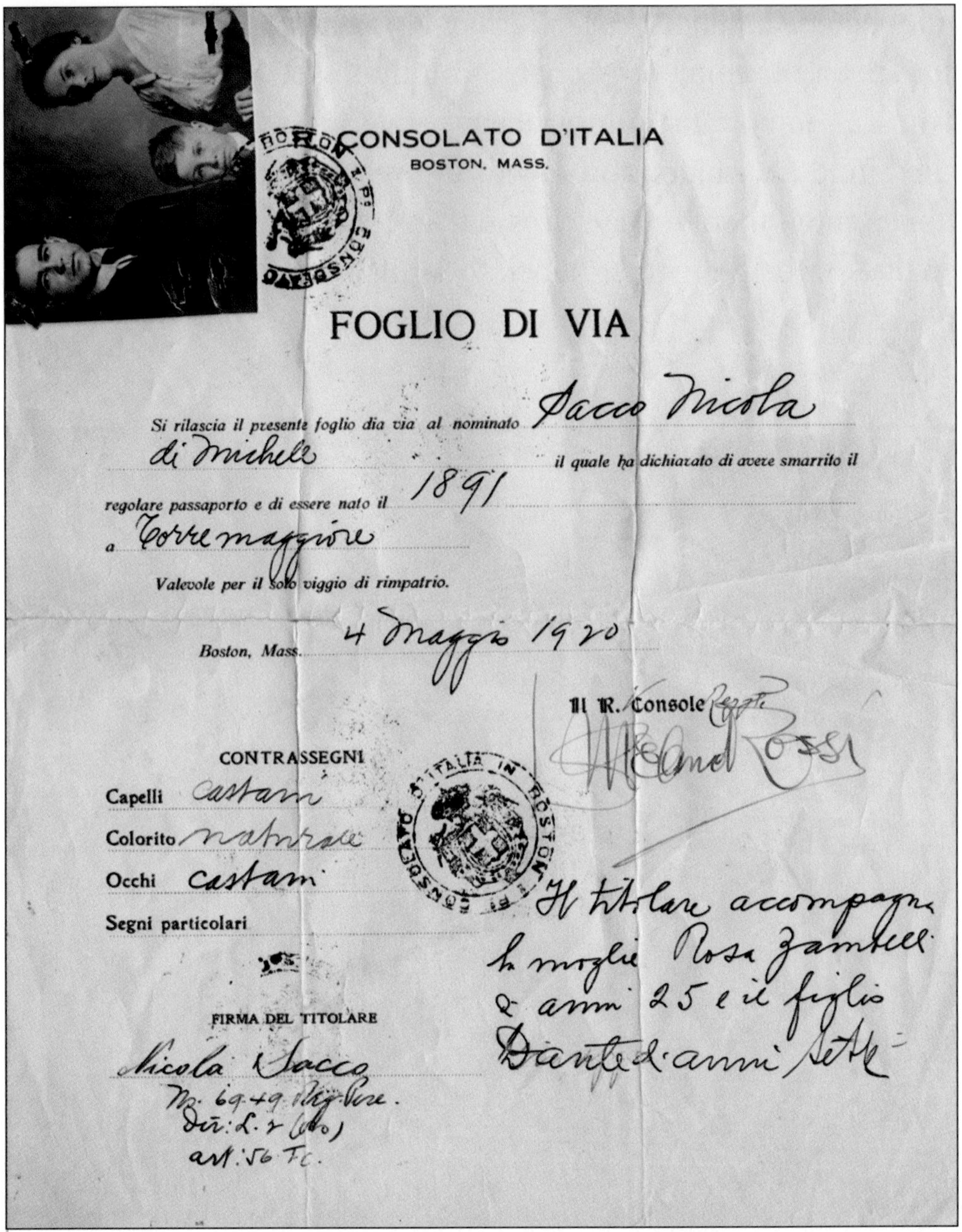

CONSOLATO D'ITALIA
BOSTON, MASS.

FOGLIO DI VIA

Si rilascia il presente foglio dia via al nominato Sacco Nicola
di Michele 1891 *il quale ha dichiarato di avere smarrito il*
regolare passaporto e di essere nato il
a Torremaggiore

Valevole per il solo viggio di rimpatrio.

Boston, Mass. 4 Maggio 1920

Il R. Console Reggente

CONTRASSEGNI

Capelli castani
Colorito naturale
Occhi castani
Segni particolari

Il titolare accompagna la moglie Rosa Zambell e anni 25 e il figlio Dante d'anni sette

FIRMA DEL TITOLARE

Nicola Sacco

Before Sacco could return to Italy, however, he needed to get a passport from the Italian Embassy in Boston. Even though Sacco could prove that he went there on April 15, that wasn't enough to save him. The police felt there still could have been enough time for him to take part in the South Braintree incident.

Things did not go smoothly for Vanzetti either. Vanzetti's line of work made it hard for him to establish where he was on the days the crimes were committed. Selling fish off a pushcart in a market meant that Vanzetti moved around a great deal. It would be hard for him to prove that he was in any one spot for very long. Therefore, Vanzetti was charged with the murders and robbery at South Braintree as well as with **"assault with intent to murder"** in the Christmas Eve Bridgewater incident. It is important to note that neither Sacco nor Vanzetti had a previous criminal record. In addition, the money taken in the South Braintree crime could not be traced to them. Yet they would soon be on trial for their lives.

Vanzetti was working his fish cart, pictured here, on the day of the robbery. This proved to be little help for his case because he moved around a great deal.

VANZETTI'S FIRST TRIAL

Vanzetti was put on trial for the attempted robbery at Bridgewater. When the trial began on June 22, 1920, in Plymouth, Massachusetts, one thing was certain: The courtroom setting was hardly desirable or even fair. Vanzetti's judge was sixty-three-year-old Webster Thayer. Thayer had a strong dislike for anarchists. Just before the trial, he had spoken harshly of a jury that found an anarchist not guilty.

TALK ABOUT THAYER

Judge Webster Thayer would later be criticized widely in the press for his disrespectful attitude in dealing with both Vanzetti and Sacco. As a *Boston Globe* reporter described Judge Thayer, "[He] was conducting himself in an undignified way, in a way I had never seen in thirty-six years . . . I have even seen the judge sit in his gown and spit on the floor."

It was Judge Webster Thayer's job to conduct a fair trial, but it soon became clear that he was prejudiced against Sacco and Vanzetti.

* * * *

The **prosecutor**, or state attorney, bringing Vanzetti to trial was Frederick G. Katzmann. Katzmann had won many cases, and was known to be good at his job.

Vanzetti's **defense lawyer**, J.P. Vahey, did the best he could. Vahey tried to show Vanzetti's whereabouts at the time of the crime. To do so, Vahey brought in a number of people who had bought fish from Vanzetti that day. If Vahey could prove that Vanzetti was busy selling and delivering fish, it would have been impossible for him to have taken part in the holdup.

Things did not go as well as Vahey hoped. Sixteen people testified in court that they had bought fish from Vanzetti that Christmas Eve, but most were unable to speak English. Even though an interpreter, or translator, was used, much of the impact of their testimony was lost. In addition, some jurors believed that "Italians always stick together," and thought that the **witnesses** were lying.

Frederick Katzmann was the prosecutor of the case.

These women testified that they had bought fish from Vanzetti on the day of the robbery.

25

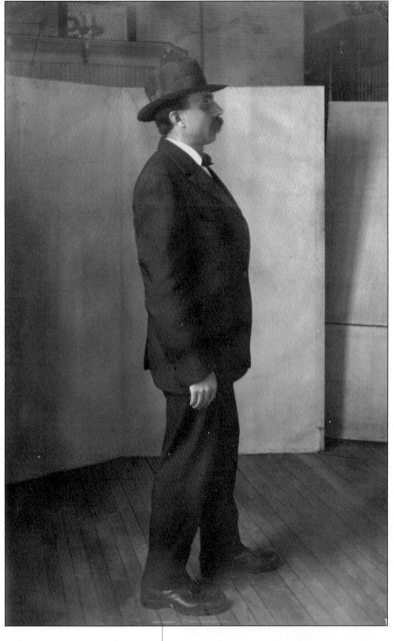

This photo of Vanzetti was taken while he was in jail.

Katzmann produced a string of witnesses as well. While these witnesses spoke English, their testimonies hardly proved that Vanzetti was the one who had committed the crime. One man said that the shooter had a neatly trimmed moustache. Vanzetti's moustache was thick and unruly. Another witness wasn't able to identify Vanzetti, but thought the criminal had been a foreigner.

The jury did not take a long time to consider the evidence. It returned a guilty **verdict** in just five and a half hours. Before sending the jurors home, Thayer said, "You may go to your homes with the feeling that you did respond as the soldier responded to his service when he went across the seas to the call of the Commonwealth." Thayer's feelings toward Vanzetti became even more obvious when the punishment was handed out. Most people **convicted** of armed robbery get eight to ten years in prison. Thayer gave Vanzetti twelve to fifteen years.

*   *   *   *

The trial was hard on Vanzetti, but his time in court was not yet over. Almost one year later, on May 31, 1921, he went on trial for the South Braintree robbery and murders. Charged with the same crime, Nicola Sacco was tried along with him.

THE SACCO & VANZETTI TRIAL

This time around, Vanzetti was defended by Jeremiah J. and Thomas F. McAnarney, two attorneys who were also brothers. The pair had an older brother, John, who was thought to be the best lawyer of the three. However, at the time of the trial, John was too busy with other clients to take the case.

This photograph shows Sacco and Vanzetti leaving the jail on their way to the courthouse.

A WORLD APART

The Sacco and Vanzetti trial was held in Dedham, Massachusetts. People accused of a crime are supposed to be tried by a jury of their peers, or people like themselves. But it would be hard to find people like Sacco and Vanzetti in Dedham. Most of the residents there were fairly wealthy and had traditional values. There were no Italians or workers similar to Sacco and Vanzetti on the jury. In addition, some members of the jury were chosen by the local sheriff's deputies. Those people were more likely to agree with the police department's view of the situation.

Fred H. Moore made many mistakes during the trial, which did little to help Sacco's case.

Sacco's lawyer was a Californian named Fred H. Moore. Moore was known for defending political radicals, but, unfortunately, he had little experience with the Massachusetts legal system. Moore did not know the Commonwealth's laws and court procedures. Many years later, in 1983, it was revealed that Moore was a drug addict. He had been secretly supplied with drugs throughout the trial, and this might have affected his ability to defend Sacco.

During the actual trial, Katzmann, who served as the prosecutor once again, brought in a number of witnesses. However, there were serious problems with some of their testimonies. Mary Splaine, a bookkeeper at the Slater and Morrill Shoe factories, swore that she saw Sacco leaning out of the getaway car's window at the railroad tracks. However, at an earlier hearing, she had been unable to identify him. When asked about the difference in her stories, Splaine denied what she had said earlier and insisted she had seen Sacco. Yet her words from the first hearing were on record.

Lewis Pelser, another witness, claimed that he also saw Sacco in the getaway car. However, he later broke down and admitted he hadn't seen anything. He'd become frightened

This photograph of the crime scene was used during trial.

and hid beneath a work bench. There were other problems with prosecution witnesses as well. Some said that the criminals spoke without accents, while both Sacco and Vanzetti had heavy Italian accents.

Testimony involving the bullets used in the shooting was shaky as well. A total of six bullets were recovered from the bodies of the victims. Captain Proctor of the Massachusetts

State Police said that the bullet that killed one of the men could have come from Sacco's gun. He later admitted that he wasn't sure about this, but the prosecution asked the question to make it sound as though he were. Meanwhile, an expert witness for the defense testified that the bullets fired at the crime scene did not come from Sacco's gun.

The bullets used in the shooting were introduced as evidence for the prosecution during the trial. One witness stated that they could have come from Sacco's gun.

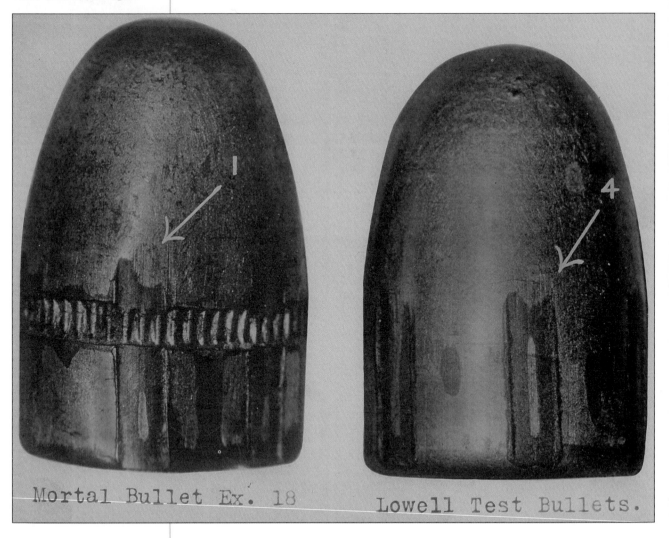

Mortal Bullet Ex. 18   Lowell Test Bullets.

* * * *

Finally, prosecutor Katzmann argued that the pair simply looked guilty. He asked the jury to examine their actions. Both men were armed when they were arrested. Both had lied about their friends and about how they had gotten their guns. Katzmann also made certain that the pair was questioned about their anarchist views and activities.

At one point during the trial, it became obvious that the jury was not being fair. As they talked about the case, one member of the jury suggested that Sacco and Vanzetti might be innocent. Another juror replied, "They ought to hang anyway." Judge Webster Thayer's prejudice was even more obvious. He continually overruled the defense attorneys' objections. As in Vanzetti's first trial, the judge's decisions favored the prosecution. Also, Sacco and Vanzetti could not speak English well, and it was hard for them to make their points in broken English. As a result, the jury found it difficult to like them or even to believe them.

It took the jury less than a day to arrive at a decision. On July 14, 1921, Nicola Sacco and Bartolomeo Vanzetti

A crowd of people gathered at the courthouse, waiting for a verdict.

ANOTHER SIDE

Some members of the public strongly believed in the defendants' innocence. Mike Kelly, the owner of the 3-K Shoe Factory in Stoughton, Massachusetts, was Sacco's employer. He thought highly of Sacco and said so. "A man who is in his garden at 4 o'clock in the morning and at the factory at 7 o'clock, and in his garden again after supper raising vegetables to give to the poor, that man is not a 'holdup man.'"

These protestors in London, England, were some of the many people around the world who protested the convictions of Sacco and Vanzetti.

were found guilty of murder and armed robbery. Both men would pay for the crime with their lives.

AN INTERNATIONAL REACTION

The trial's unfairness upset people around the world. Angry protests and demonstrations were held in the United States and abroad. People everywhere pointed to the flimsy evidence on which the men were convicted. Even celebrities became involved in the case. The famous scientist Albert Einstein spoke out against the way the men had been treated. The same was true for well-known writers, such as Dorothy Parker and Thomas Mann. Numerous other stars also favored having a new trial for Sacco and Vanzetti.

* * * *

Many people began to take hope that the men would be saved in an **appeal**. During an appeal, attorneys ask for a court's decision to be reviewed or for a new trial to take place. Usually, appeals are granted if it is determined that an error was made in the case the first time it was tried. Sacco and Vanzetti's appeals were handled by new lawyers. This time, the highly regarded attorney William G. Thompson came to their defense, assisted by Herbert B. Ehrmann.

The lawyers argued that the verdict was unfair because of bias (prejudice) on the jury's part. Thompson also stressed that the verdict did not truly represent the evidence. These defense lawyers even produced new witnesses for their clients. The statements given by these people were the opposite of what was said by the prosecution's witnesses.

This photograph shows Sacco and Vanzetti, handcuffed, being taken to Superior Court for their appeal.

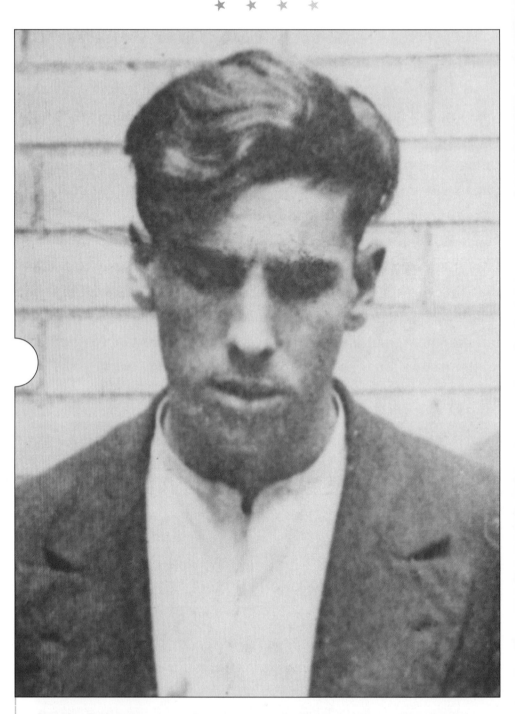

Celestino F. Medeiros eventually confessed to the South Braintree robbery, but his confession was not enough to save Sacco and Vanzetti.

✳ ✳ ✳ ✳

Though Thompson and Ehrmann brought up some important points, their efforts did not amount to anything. Judge Thayer also served as the appeals judge, and it was unlikely that Thayer would rule against his own actions. As expected, all of Sacco's and Vanzetti's appeals were turned down. By October 1, 1924, Judge Thayer had denied six such motions put forth by the defense.

However, in 1925, the men's verdict was appealed for a very important reason. On November 18, Celestino F. Medeiros, who was already in jail for killing a bank cashier in an unrelated crime, sent a note to Sacco. It stated the following: "I hereby confess to being in the South Braintree shoe company crime and Sacco and Vanzetti was not in said crime."

The confession made sense. Medeiros had been part of the Morelli Gang, a group of Italian Americans known for robbing freight cars. The gang leader, Joe Morelli, looked very much

Joe Morelli, shown here in a police mug shot, was the leader of a group of professional criminals called the Morelli Gang. The gang had previously stolen shoes—including those of Slater and Morrill—from freight cars.

like Sacco. Yet when Thompson and Ehrmann raised these points in a new appeal, Judge Thayer decided that the confession was unreliable.

In April 1927, the Massachusetts Supreme Judicial Court, the Commonwealth's highest court, upheld Thayer's ruling on the appeal. It ruled that the judge had not made any errors in the trial or abused his power. Sacco's and Vanzetti's lawyers even went to the nation's highest court, the United States Supreme Court. However, the Court refused to hear the case.

It looked like the end of the line for Sacco and Vanzetti. On April 9, 1927, Judge Thayer sentenced them to death. Desperate to save their clients, the men's lawyers went to Massachusetts governor Alvan T. Fuller to stop the executions.

On June 1, 1927, Fuller appointed a group of people to handle the matter. Known as the Lowell Commission, its members would review the facts surrounding the case. Unfortunately, the commission was made up of men who shared many of Judge Thayer's prejudices. On July 27, 1927, the Lowell Commission delivered a report to Governor Fuller stating that the trail had been fair. After that, the governor decided not to stop the executions.

Governor Alvan T. Fuller was under a great deal of pressure from the public to review the facts of Sacco's and Vanzetti's case. Supporters of the convicted men sent many letters asking for Fuller's help.

36

On August 29, 1927, thousands of people took part in the funeral processions of Sacco and Vanzetti.

THEIR LEGACY

Nicola Sacco and Bartolomeo Vanzetti were executed on August 23, 1927. Both died in the electric chair, claiming their innocence to the end. In the days prior to their executions, there were protests in a number of major cities. Afterwards, thousands marched in their funeral procession.

Some supporters saw Sacco and Vanzetti as heroes who died for their beliefs. A number of people were furious at the legal system. Within months, the home of the executioner was bombed. In September 1932, Judge Thayer's home was bombed as well. No one was hurt in either case, but the judge moved elsewhere.

This photograph shows Judge Thayer's home after the bombing.

* * * *

Novels, plays, and poems were written about Sacco and Vanzetti. The men may have died, but their story would not. Over time, even the Commonwealth of Massachusetts was forced to admit that Sacco and Vanzetti had been denied a fair trial. As a result, a new law was passed in Massachusetts: Chapter 341 of the Acts of 1939. This law granted more power to the Massachusetts Supreme Judicial Court to address injustices within the legal system such as the ones Sacco and Vanzetti experienced.

The law allowed the court to order a new trial if new evidence was discovered after the jury reached a decision. Under the new law, the court could also order a new trial if a jury's decision was not supported by the evidence. Other states passed similar laws.

As time passed, Sacco and Vanzetti were not forgotten. Fifty years after their deaths, Massachusetts governor Michael Dukakis proclaimed August 23, 1977, "Nicola Sacco and Bartolomeo Vanzetti Memorial Day." Declaring that "any stigma and disgrace should be forever removed from their names," Dukakis called on people not to forget these men. He urged everyone to make sure that

THE BENEFITS OF A TRAGEDY

Before his death, Vanzetti said that he hoped the injustice he and Sacco endured would help others. He noted, "If it had not been for these things, I might have lived out my life talking at street corners to scorning men. I might have died unmarked, unknown, a failure. Now we are not a failure. This [our wrongful conviction] is our career and our triumph. Never in our full life could we hope to do such work for tolerance, for justice, for man's understanding of man as now we do by accident."

Gutzon Borglum's memorial to Sacco and Vanzetti features the two men facing a tilted scale of justice, which represents the lack of justice in their case, and Vanzetti's final words.

"the forces of intolerance, fear, and hatred" never again overtake the legal system.

Sacco and Vanzetti were again remembered in 1997 on the seventieth anniversary of their deaths. This time, Thomas Menino, Boston's Italian American mayor, dedicated a

HAT I WISH MORE THAN ALL, IN THIS LAST HOUR OF AGONY, IS THAT OUR CASE AND OUR FATE MAY BE UNDERSTOOD IN THEIR REAL BEING AND SERVE AS A TREMENDOUS LESSON TO THE FORCES OF FREEDOM SO THAT OUR SUFFERING AND DEATH WILL NOT HAVE BEEN IN VAIN

memorial—a bronze sculpture done by Gutzon Borglum in 1927—to the men. The mayor placed the statue in Boston as the city's tribute to Sacco and Vanzetti—two men denied justice in a nation based on liberty and justice for all.

Glossary

anarchists—people who are against any form of government

appeal—challenging a lower court's decision in a higher court

assault with intent to murder—to attack someone intending to kill him or her

communist—a society in which the government distributes property and power equally among all people

convicted—determined to be guilty of a crime

defense lawyer—attorney who represents a person who is on trial

deportation—the process of having an immigrant permanently removed from a country

ethnicity—cultural background, such as Italian

immigrants—people who have come to a new country to live permanently

paymaster—person in charge of paying the employees of a business

prejudice—an opinion (usually negative) that is formed about someone or something without any basis in fact

prosecutor—attorney for the government who brings those believed to be guilty of crimes to trial

suspects—people who are thought to have committed a crime

traitors—people who are accused of betraying their country

verdict—a jury's decision

witnesses—people who have seen or heard something relevant to a crime

Timeline: Sacco and

1919

DECEMBER 24
A holdup attempt takes place in Bridgewater, Massachusetts.

1920

APRIL 15
In a robbery in South Braintree, Massachusetts, two men are killed and nearly $16,000 is stolen.

MAY 5
Sacco and Vanzetti are arrested.

JUNE 22
Vanzetti goes on trial for the attempted Bridgewater robbery.

1921

MAY 31
Sacco and Vanzetti go on trial for the robbery and murders at South Braintree, Massachusetts.

JULY 14
Sacco and Vanzetti are found guilty of the robbery and murders at South Braintree, Massachusetts.

1925

NOVEMBER 18
Celestino F. Medeiros sends a note to Sacco confessing to the South Braintree robbery and murders.

APRIL 9
Sacco and Vanzetti are sentenced to die by electrocution.

1927

JUNE 1
Governor Alvan T. Fuller forms the Lowell Commission to review the Sacco and Vanzetti case

Vanzetti

JULY 27
The Lowell Commission delivers a report to Governor Fuller supporting the guilty verdict in the Sacco and Vanzetti case.

SEPTEMBER 27
Judge Thayer's home is bombed.

AUGUST 23
Boston mayor Thomas Menino dedicates a bronze sculpture as a memorial to Sacco and Vanzetti.

AUGUST 23
Sacco and Vanzetti are executed.

AUGUST 23
Governor Michael Dukakis proclaims August 23, 1977, to be "Nicola Sacco and Bartolomeo Vanzetti Memorial Day."

SAVE SACCO & VANZETTI

PROTEST DEMONSTRATION AGAINST DEATH SENTENCE

HYDE PARK WEDNESDAY 10 AT 7 PM

COME IN YOUR THOUSANDS

45

To Find Out More

BOOKS

Downing, David. *Communism*. Chicago, Illinois: Heinemann Library, 2003.

Hinton, Kerry. *The Trial of Sacco and Vanzetti: A Primary Source Account*. New York, NY: Rosen Publishing Group, 2003.

Hoobler, Dorothy and Thomas Hoobler. *The Italian American Family Album*. Oxford, UK: Oxford University Press Children's Books, 1998.

ONLINE SITES

Spartacus Educational: Sacco and Vanzetti Case
www.spartacus.schoolnet.co.uk/USAsacco.htm

Court TV—The Greatest Trials of All Time
http://www.courttv.com/archive/greatesttrials/sacco.vanzetti/

Index

Bold numbers indicate illustrations.

About the Author

Award-winning children's book author **Elaine Landau** worked as a newspaper reporter, a children's book editor, and a youth services librarian before becoming a full-time writer. She has written more than two hundred books for young readers. Landau lives in Miami, Florida, with her husband, Norman, and their son, Michael.